Mindfulness for Beginners

Improve Mental Health and Find Peace Everyday

(How to Live in the Moment While Becoming Stress and Worry Free Forever)

Charles Hester

Published by Rob Miles

© **Charles Hester**

All Rights Reserved

Mindfulness for Beginners: Improve Mental Health and Find Peace Everyday (How to Live in the Moment While Becoming Stress and Worry Free Forever)

ISBN 978-1-989990-86-5

All rights reserved. No part of this guide may be reproduced in any form without permission in writing from the publisher except in the case of brief quotations embodied in critical articles or reviews.

Legal & Disclaimer

The information contained in this book is not designed to replace or take the place of any form of medicine or professional medical advice. The information in this book has been provided for educational and entertainment purposes only.

The information contained in this book has been compiled from sources deemed reliable, and it is accurate to the best of the Author's knowledge; however, the Author cannot guarantee its accuracy and validity and cannot be held liable for any errors or omissions. Changes are periodically made to this book. You must consult your doctor or get professional medical advice before using any of the suggested remedies, techniques, or information in this book.

Upon using the information contained in this book, you agree to hold harmless the Author from and against any damages, costs, and expenses, including any legal fees potentially resulting from the application of any of the information provided by this guide. This disclaimer applies to any damages or injury caused by the use and application, whether directly or indirectly, of any advice or information presented, whether for breach of contract, tort, negligence, personal injury, criminal intent, or under any other cause of action.

You agree to accept all risks of using the information presented inside this book. You need to consult a professional medical practitioner in order to ensure you are both able and healthy enough to participate in this program.

Table of Contents

INTRODUCTION 1

CHAPTER 1: STRESS AND YOUR SUBCONSCIOUS AND CONSCIOUS MIND 3

CHAPTER 2: THE RELEVANCE OF NOW 7

CHAPTER 3: WHAT IS MINDFULNESS? 18

CHAPTER 4: WHAT IS MINDFULNESS? 47

CHAPTER 5: THE BENEFITS OF MINDFUL MEDITATION 64

CHAPTER 6: SECRETS OF FLOW 71

CHAPTER 7: IMPROVING GENERAL HEALTH 84

CHAPTER 8: BENEFITS OF MINDFULNESS 94

CHAPTER 9: PUTTING WORDS INTO POWER AND PERSPECTIVE 99

CHAPTER 10: MINDFULNESS EXERCISES THROUGH RELAXATION AND EFFORTS. 106

CHAPTER 11: INCORPORATING MINDFULNESS IN OTHER ROUTINE ACTIVITIES.. 115

CHAPTER 12: CALM THE FEELINGS................................. 134

CHAPTER 13: PRACTICING MEDITATION 155

CHAPTER 14: MINDFULNESS WITH FOOD 163

CHAPTER 15: MINDFUL WALKING 179

CONCLUSION.. 190

Introduction

You are about to learn proven steps and strategies on how to relieve stress through mindfulness-based exercises. These exercises are simple and you can easily do on your own.

This guide has been designed for anyone who is trying to find ways on how to cope with daily anxiety and stress in a healthy way, without having to take medication or even go to the spa.

Mindfulness based stress reduction techniques, or MBSR, has been one of the growing fields of psychology and physical therapy that has been helping millions of people deal with life's pressures simply by allowing them to be aware of their own body, state of mind, and environment.

Many clinical studies conducted have found that those who are doing MBSR are able to take advantage of many benefits, including relieving stress and building resilience to life's daily stressors in way that they can remain relaxed despite pressure.

If you are one of those people who need a way to deal with stress the natural and spiritual way, this is a book made for you.

Thanks again for choosing this guide!

Let's get started...

Chapter 1: Stress And Your Subconscious And Conscious Mind

Most times, when a difficult situation such as a conflict or an argument arises, you can operate on autopilot, without really thinking about the situation at hand. Behaviors and thoughts often emanate from emotions that, if you fail to apply conscious control over, can keep running through your subconscious mind. Your subconscious mind continues to process all of the things going on in your life.

Most of the things we do are under the control of our autopilot mind. For instance, you wake up every morning, go to use the bathroom, fix breakfast, catch the morning news, and follow the same route to work without consciously thinking about any of these things. These actions, like several others, are ones you have done so repeatedly that they have registered in your subconscious mind to a point where you can now do them without any conscious thought or being mindful of them at all.

The same goes for negative self-talk and thoughts that cause stress. Even your breathing follows the same autopilot route—though you can breathe both subconsciously and consciously—but until you become mindful enough to pay attention to your breathing, which you learn to do through mindful meditation, breathing remains a subconscious activity controlled by your autopilot mind.

The amazing thing about breathing is that it creates a deep connection between your conscious and subconscious mind. This is why mindfulness techniques that require mindful breathing are a good way to deal with issues such as high stress levels, depression and anxiety fueled by past negative experiences, fears of the future, negative self-beliefs, poor health conditions, unhealthy relationships, poor sleeping and eating habits, and toxic work environment etc.

The fact that we live in a world and age where we have several things that can increase your stress level even without you noticing how much damage stress is causing you does not help matters. Stress from work, home, your relationship, financial problems, health-related issues, insecurity issues, traffic, and from several other sources can cause depressive thoughts to invade your mind.

Reversing this stress will require lots of mindful practices and positive habits to make sure your subconscious mind receives healthy information that can induce positive behaviors.

Before we look at how you can start this practice, let us see some ways stress affects different aspects of your life:

Chapter 2: The Relevance Of Now

If you take an eggcup and fill it with a pint of boiling water, the water will overspill, and you will likely scald yourself in the process. It would be a foolish thing to do. However, it is what we do to our minds every day of the week. We fill the mind with aspects of our past, worries about the future and all kinds of thoughts. These can be considered as the boiling waters of the mind because those thoughts are very volatile indeed. In the fraction of a second, we can jump back to an event in the past and feel that hurt again. If you can imagine the mind as being split into different sections, a disciplined mind can close the various boxes and keep things in order.

However, for most people, this isn't even an option. Thoughts are random. They come and go. We relive the hurts of the past, and we tend to spend a lot of our time in retrospective thought. Imagine the state of the boxes within the mind when we keep on digging up more thoughts from the past. It would be very much like the eggcup overflowing and will certainly cause an element of confusion, anxiety and pain. Thus, mindfulness tackles this very neatly. It will take a little while before you can live in the now.

In the 21st century, we are so accustomed to multi-tasking and have the impression that it's pretty neat to be able to do that. In fact, the brain wasn't built to multi-task. Scientists did a study on multi-tasking and found that more efficiency was gained if one job was tackled at a time and finished. However, if you have kids screaming and the TV set blaring, as well as someone knocking on the door, we automatically go into multi-tasking mode and are not getting the best out of our lives. Amid all of this, we have problems from the past that may have left their scars, leaving us anxious or even having self-esteem issues and when a moment of peace happens – we dig into the past – either for good memories or to indulge in feeling sorry for ourselves. The negative thoughts that build up are unhealthy. They equate to re-introducing bad things into our lives. Why would people do that? The fact is that people do that because it's what they know. What they need to learn is a new approach based on discipline, and that's where mindfulness comes in.

Inside your head, you have your conscious voice and your subconscious, and they both deal with things in different ways. Your subconscious doesn't get confused by emotions. It simply sees and records all that happens in your life, during the hours of being awake and also when you sleep. The subconscious mind is more efficient that the conscious mind because it doesn't allow emotions to cloud its view. It can calculate things in a much quicker way than the conscious mind can. However, with the kind of lives that we live, we don't often let the subconscious mind take over. We are too busy with thoughts.

Eliminating unnecessary thoughts

For this exercise, look at the kind of thoughts that you have in the next few days and work out how much time you spend in the present moment. Chances are that you spend far too long in the past and not enough in the present moment. With mindfulness practice, you get to cut out all the interference from the past and the future by seeing the thought, recognizing it but not judging it and then simply pulling yourself back into the present moment. If you are so busy living in the past, your present moment doesn't count for much because you didn't live it and that's where people are causing themselves suffering.

We look into an event that happened in the past. The emotional side of the conscious brain associates that thought with misery, and we wallow in our suffering. The subconscious mind merely sees a chain of events. Sad thought – sadness following it. It, therefore, assumes that the normal course of events means when you think about the past, it makes you unhappy. All of this information is stored, so that when the same event happens again, the subconscious knows that your response to this kind of thought is going to be negative. It's the same with all angry thoughts, and this includes:

Jealousy

Hate

Greed

Anger

In fact, any negative retrospective memory that you allow to go through your head will be seen by the subconscious as producing more negativity. That's what it sees, and that is what it registers. Thus, when you decide to think about something negative, your subconscious kicks in with a negative response. It doesn't understand emotions, but it does understand reactions.

What you need to be able to do is think of this moment in time as being the only one that counts. You cannot stop thoughts from the past from happening. It is natural. However, you can use all of your senses to see those thoughts in a different light, so that your subconscious registers positive reaction instead of negative and your life becomes less stressful. So how do you react in a positive way to a negative situation from the past? That's easy with mindfulness. You observe the thought for what it is. You place no judgment on it; you acknowledge that you had the thought, and you move back to the present moment without any emotional reaction.

The relevance of NOW is all that matters. You can't stifle thoughts. They happen and although some books tell you to stifle them – that's a mistake. You need your thoughts. However, what you don't need is to dwell on them and make them into negative reactions.

Thought: My partner was unfaithful three years ago

Reaction from a Mindfulness perspective: Today is three years on. I have learned from the experience.

Exercise in Mindfulness

For the next 24 hours, every time you have a negative thought about the past or worry for the future, acknowledge it, see it for what it is without any emotions being involved and dismiss it, coming back to the moment in which you are living. It is vital that you learn to alter your response to negative triggers. By doing this, you are re-educating your mind to be able to handle bad things. You won't automatically get stressed when bad thoughts happen. You will simply acknowledge them and then dismiss them. You don't even have to have an answer to them. The past has gone. The future has not yet happened. Why let these periods of your life destroy the present moment. Acknowledge the thought, dismiss it and move back into the moment.

Exercise in distraction

Mindfulness may need a distraction to help you in the early stages when you are learning the discipline of self-control. Have something that you can concentrate on in the moment to take the place of negative thoughts about the past or future. For example, you could have a flower on your desk at work to take your attention away from the thought. Concentrate on that flower and upon its beauty. Look at each petal and each stamen and enjoy the beauty of it. In the home, perhaps you could have an inspiring image to look at to help you move through negative moment back into the present moment.

Chapter 3: What Is Mindfulness?

Mindfulness is not in any way complicated; it is a straightforward concept to understand.

Mindfulness can be defined as the art of paying attention to your present thoughts and feelings without being judgmental. The human mind has the tendency to wander; most of us can hardly focus on one task at a time. Before you decided to read this book or even while reading, there must have been a couple of thoughts that came to your mind. Some of the thoughts could be about that task that you haven't completed, something about the kids that you need to take care of, something about your relationship or other reasons why it might not be a good idea to be idling away reading a book when there are a lot of uncompleted tasks you should be taking care of instead.

Mindfulness helps you to avoid living like this and instead helps you focus on the present moment. Therefore, if you are reading this book, mindfulness helps you focus only on reading this book and not how soon you will finish reading to do something else or how you have not finished a particular task. This is beneficial because incessant thoughts can easily lead to anxiety, depression, and other mental problems.

Mindfulness helps you live a peaceful and focused life. It helps you focus on one thing at a time and helps you avoid falling into the trap of multitasking. Multitasking is a trap because contrary to what most people believe that multitasking will help save time and help them become more time efficient, studies have shown that people who concentrate on a single task at a time have better speed and accuracy compared to people who multitask.

Mindfulness also helps you to avoid missing out on your life. Many people grow old, only to discover that they missed out on precious moments of their lives either because they were worried about perfection of the moment or they were worrying about other things in the future that they did not notice and take in what was happening right before their eyes.

Mindfulness teaches you to live in the moment without regretting about the past or worrying about the future.

So, what are other benefits of learning to be mindful of your present? Let us find out:

Improves Focus - Mindfulness helps you to avoid distracting information so that you can focus better whether at work, school or when undertaking any project or activity that requires concentration.

Improves Emotional Intelligence - People with high emotional reactivity can also benefit from practicing mindfulness, as it helps you to take your time to respond to issue rather than just saying something hastily that you will regret later.

Improves Physical Health - Mindfulness can be very beneficial to your physical health in a number of ways. It helps to reduce anxiety and stress, which helps to reduce blood pressure, heart diseases, gastrointestinal difficulties and other health conditions caused by stress. It also helps you sleep better and as a result, helps you to be healthier both physically and mentally.

Improves Mental Health - Mindfulness can be very effective for treating depression, anxiety disorders, substance abuse, OCD and a number of other mental problems.

Practicing mindfulness helps you do away with behaviors and attitudes that may work against your ability to live a satisfied and fulfilled life. It helps you to avoid being caught up in regrets about the past or worries about the future such that you don't see what is happening now. It also helps you improve your relationships since each time you are with a loved one, you are completely "there" with them, and your mind does not have a million thoughts.

MINDFULNESS TECHNIQUES

Mindfulness can be classified into two major types; Informal and formal mindfulness.

Formal mindfulness is what most people refer to as mindfulness meditation. It involves deliberately taking time to practice mindfulness consciously while informal mindfulness involves incorporating the practice of mindfulness into your daily life and activities such that mindfulness now becomes a part of you.

Both types of mindfulness are very important and essential for you if you truly want to live a mindful life. You cannot do without one or the other; each one supports the other and both have to be practiced hand in hand.

Formal Mindfulness

As mentioned earlier, formal mindfulness entails taking some time daily to practice mindfulness consciously. This kind of mindfulness helps to increase your concentration and to live in the moment. It helps you discover that the secret of well-being is learning to live in the moment. Think of it as a kind of 'holiday' or 'break' from your daily life where you have to think about many things and do many things at a time.

When you practice formal mindfulness, you are able to take a break (even if it is for a few minutes) from your constantly wandering mind to enjoy the present moment and this is one of the keys to well-being. Further, the more you practice mindfulness meditation, the easier it becomes to be mindful in your daily activities and thus practicing informal mindfulness becomes much easier and mindfulness becomes a part of you.

To practice formal mindfulness, you would need to set apart a particular time of the day and a place where you can do your meditation. This could be in the mornings before breakfast, during lunch break at work or any other time that is most suitable for you. You would need a lot of discipline to make this work because you would have to do it at the same time every day.

Let us look at the various types of formal mindfulness techniques that you can practice to learn to be more mindful:

Body Scan Meditation

This type of meditation involves becoming conscious of the sensations and movements within your body. It helps you to discover the way your thoughts and attention drifts easily and helps you to learn how to be less judgmental towards yourself when your mind wanders.

It also helps you to become aware of the different parts of your body and the different regions therein. You are able to fully experience how each body part feels while releasing the pent-up emotions and sense of urgency towards uncompleted tasks.

Some of the benefits you can derive from body scan meditation include:

Improved focus

Helps you shift your attention from worries and troubling thoughts

Helps you relax and release negative emotions that may have built up within your body.

Helps you switch to 'relax mode'

You can practice body scan meditation in any desired position; sitting, standing or lying but the most recommended position is lying down.

How to Do Body Scan Meditation

Set aside 15 – 20 minutes to practice every day.

Choose a quiet place where you will not be undisturbed.

Switch off your phone or put it in 'silent mode'.

Lie on your back with your arms a little bit away from the sides of your body and your legs a little apart from each other so they don't touch. Make sure the temperature in the room and your lying position feels comfortable enough.

Let go of any ideas of perfection, self-improvement or other thoughts regarding personal development; let your mind just be free.

Direct your attention to your breaths and observe your breathing pattern for a few minutes.

Begin to scan your body, starting from your toes. Focus your attention on your toes and observe how they feel. Does they feel hot or cold? Observe the sensations in your toes and don't judge them. Don't try to classify them as good or bad; just become aware of them.

From your toes, move to your feet and observe the sensations there too. Move to other parts of your body following this sequence:

Your feet

Upper and lower legs

Pelvic area

Upper and lower torso

Shoulders

Upper and lower arms

Hands

Neck

Face

Back of your head

Top of your head

Just continue to observe each part of your body until you get to the top of your head.

Note that your attention may drift as you do it but don't judge yourself, just slowly direct your attention back to your breathing each time it drifts; observe your breathing pattern and imagine your breaths going in and out of your body then slowly, direct your attention back to where you stopped.

When you are done scanning your entire body, just relax for a few minutes while letting go of all thoughts and emotions.

Don't get up hurriedly when you are done, slowly bring your meditation to a close and stand up slowly to avoid feeling dizzy or falling down.

Movement or Walking Meditation

Walking or movement meditation as is sometimes called, is one of the ways through which you can bring mindfulness into your daily activities as it helps you to be more present in your body and in the present moment. It involves paying attention to the way you feel as you move because most of the time when you walk, you are hardly paying attention to your body. Your mind will mostly be engaged in other things like imagining, planning, or worrying about various things. However, when you practice walking meditation, you are able to move your attention from the outside world to what is happening within your body.

Walking/movement meditation is different from sitting meditation because you have to keep your eyes open when doing movement meditation. While you can practice movement or walking meditation anywhere, it is best practiced outdoors. Before we learn how to practice walking meditation, you may want to know some benefits of walking meditation. Let us find out in the next section:

Benefits of Walking Meditation

It helps you to connect more deeply with your environment. As you walk, you become aware of everything around you; the earth beneath the soles of your feet, the air flowing in and out of your lungs, the smell, the sounds and sights and everything around you. This creates more situational awareness and helps you understand that you are part of the environment you live in.

It helps to clear mental fog. It does this by breaking a rigid and constant train of thoughts and helps you to open your mind up to newer and better perspectives.

It provides you an opportunity to commune with nature. If you believe in prayer, it is a great time to pray and dialogue with nature.

It helps you to connect with, and understand your body better. It establishes a deeper connection between your mind and body.

It helps you to slow down a racing and distressed mind.

It improves your ability to concentrate.

It increases your ability to live a mindful life and connect to the present moment.

How to do Walking/Movement Meditation

Look for a pathway to do your walking meditation. This pathway should be about 30 to 40 feet long and one that allows you to walk back and forth easily. You could also use circular movements but the disadvantage with walking in a circle is that it can sometimes conceal a wandering mind compared to walking back and forth where once you stop at the end of a path and turn around, you would be able to easily detect and refocus your wandering mind.

Keep your eye on the path you are walking through. Avoid looking at anything in particular to avoid distractions.

Start your walking meditation with standing on a spot at the beginning of your walking path. As you stand, take note of the way the weight of your body is transferred to your feet and then to the earth.

Begin to walk back and forth on this single path. Walk at a pace that sets you at ease. Don't walk too slowly or too fast, just choose a pace that allows your mind to be calm and alert. You can also try to alternate your speed.

When you've found the perfect pace, direct your attention to your lower legs and your feet and begin to feel the sensations in your body as you take each step.

Notice the tension in your legs and your feet as you lift each leg and the way your leg moves through the air and comes in contact with the ground.

Mentally label your steps as you would label your left and right foot as they move. This helps to occupy your mind so that you can avoid wandering.

Let go of any other thoughts and emotions that have nothing to do with walking and focus on walking.

As you walk, you should try to avoid any distracting sights but if you find anything attractive such that it is difficult not to look at it, stop for a few minutes and observe that sight; you could do a few seconds of looking meditation and then continue with your walking meditation.

As you walk, continue to be aware of the sensations in your feet and then move to your ankles and joints. Notice the sensations in them as you walk. Move your attention from your ankles to your shin and then your calves, knees, thighs, hips, pelvis, belly, chest, lower arms, upper arms, elbows, wrists, forearms, hands and fingers. Move on to your neck and then your chin, your jaws and eyes. Notice the sensations and feelings in each part.

Now, take note of your emotions. Don't label them as bad or good, don't cling to them or try to push them away, simple acknowledge that they are there as you continue to move.

Try to balance your inner and outer experience. As you walk, your environment would feel calm and maybe, quiet. Try to bring this same calmness into your body and mind.

You are about to bring the session to a close now but you shouldn't just halt rapidly, you have to tell yourself that you are stopping in a few seconds and then stop. When you stop, stand for a few minutes, and direct your attention back to the way your weight feels on the soles of your feet.

Bring the session to a close slowly. You should feel more relaxed and calm at this point. You can go on with your daily activities at this point.

Breathing Space Meditation

Breathing space meditation is one of the most commonly taught forms of meditation in the practice of mindfulness. It is made of three major parts: Awareness inwards, breath, and consciously expanding.

The benefits of practicing breathing space meditation are similar to those of the other types of meditation mentioned above.

Let us look at the three major parts of breathing space meditation

Awareness Inwards: This allows you to become more aware of your physical sensations, your thoughts, as well as your emotions.

Breath: It helps you to study and become aware of your breathing patterns as a way to bring your mind to focus.

Consciously Expanding: This one expands your attention on the sensations in your body as well as your breathing patterns.

The breathing space meditation can be performed in three minutes, that is why it is sometimes called the three minutes meditation but this doesn't necessarily mean that you have to do it for three minutes. You can do it for as long as you like, depending on your current location and how much time you have to spare.

How to do Breathing Space Meditation

1. Look for a calm, quiet place where you will be free from distractions.

2. Look for a chair with a sturdy back and sit upright or in a position where you don't have to strain your back or your neck. You can also choose an upright standing or lying position but it is better to sit up straight in order to improve communication with the brain.

3. Start with Step A; remember, there are three steps so if you want to do it for three minutes, you will need to dedicate a minute to doing each step.

Step A

Become aware of your body sensations, aches, pains, pleasant and unpleasant feelings. Just observe them without judgments.

Become aware of your emotions; your heart, your belly and other areas where you can feel emotions. Again, just observe and do not judge.

Become aware of the thoughts going through your mind. Observe each thought as it comes and goes without judgments.

4. Move on to step B

Step B

Start by focusing your attention on your lower abdomen.

Observe your breath as air flows in and out of your body.

Observe any changes in the rate of your breath.

5. Move on to step C

Step C

Start by directing your awareness to your belly.

Gradually move to the other parts of your body and continue to observe how energy flows from one part to another.

Slowly end your breathing space meditation.

Informal Mindfulness

Informal mindfulness entails living a life of mindfulness; practicing mindfulness in every aspect of your life and in everything, you do. It involves practicing mindfulness in your sitting, walking, breathing, eating, reading, working and basically, everything you do.

This type of mindfulness is essential for you to enjoy the benefits of practicing mindfulness, as it helps you to completely focus and commit yourself to anything you are doing presently. Informal mindfulness can be likened to the sea; as the sea settles, the water becomes clearer just in the same way your mind becomes clearer as you practice informal mindfulness.

Before you can learn how to incorporate mindfulness into your daily activities, you will need to consciously practice mindfulness (formal mindfulness). Over time, practicing mindfulness in everything you do will become almost automatic.

Chapter 4: What Is Mindfulness?

Mindfulness can help transform you into a better, happier, and healthier version of yourself. Some of the many benefits associated with mindfulness are happiness, awareness, ability to focus on the good things, and more! Mindfulness is not limited to just your actions or routine - - it involves your thoughts, your imaginations, your soul, and your feelings. There is energy around that you can use positively or negatively, depending on how you feel. If you're sad about something, everything will appear dull; when you're euphoric, everything from weather to people seems happy and bright. Your inner feelings dominate your outer surroundings, influencing how you perceive the world.

To find new happiness in your life, you don't need outside help. You're the reason for everything in your life, and your existence is a miracle. Focusing on things that are out of your control distracts from real happiness and can lead to anxiety. True happiness is generated from within your heart -- all you need to do is to find it. Living in the present without worrying about your past and your future is one way of striving for that goal.

There are only a few prerequisites for mindfulness. Anyone can experience it and use it for better living by simply being "present" in the moment. Forget about the past and the future, since you can't control them. If you've done all you reasonably can to prepare, worrying won't help, so don't let events you can't change control your happiness and sadness. Constantly planning and worrying prevents you from enjoying the moment, making you unable to even enjoy a cup of coffee without being haunted by worries of the unforeseen.

Mindfulness lets you notice the little things in life that make you happy and relaxed. For example, when you're walking in a park and thinking about which bills you have to pay, how can you expect to be happy? How can you enjoy the green grass, the infectious laughter of children playing, or the beautiful sound of birds singing? Live in the moment; peaceful moments are rare. There are so many worries in life that it's hard to be happy, so if you miss an opportunity to enjoy nature, there's no guarantee another moment will come along soon.

The human mind is notorious for wandering to topics that worry you, but mindfulness tricks can change your course of thinking to make yours a happy mind. You can't control your future and whatever will be, will be, but at least you can change your perspective. Select the positive aspects of your life to focus on while letting go of your fears. Worries take you away from the present, and leave you nothing but sadness and distress.

How to be Mindful

Mindfulness is not a destination, but a journey!

Mindfulness is a long-term goal that can bring many positive changes to your life. You may feel sad at times when you forget about the things that are important in your life. The reason for this is not that your mind is weak and forgetful, but because you're thinking about the things that stress you too much. Many people constantly think about their fears and regrets, missing out on the moment they're actually living in, and staying stuck in their personal fears. This attitude prevents you from being mindful and present.

The real meaning of mindfulness is connecting your body, your soul, and your thoughts. When your thoughts are not under your control, you cannot be mindful. Happiness will not come like this, but when you focus on the moment you're living in, and your soul is present with your mind and body. There are many ways to become mindful, all of which are enjoyable and easy to follow.

You don't need to consciously make an effort to become happy, but when you are not mindful, try hard to enjoy the moment. When you do, you'll forget your worries, and happiness will surround you. Find a place that gives you peace and happiness when you are focusing on being mindful: sit in your backyard or a garden to search for your inner joy. This is a step-by-step process in which every step towards mindfulness leads you closer to joy and peace.

When you're focusing on your inner self, you stop talking to others or worrying about things beyond your control. By focusing on yourself and your inner emotions, you can listen to the voices in your heart and calm them down in an attempt to be peaceful. When you concentrate, you will find ways to keep yourself happy and satisfied.

Life is a constant blend of happiness and stress, and you only have control of a fraction of the events around you. However, you can always control yourself, and decide that nothing will decrease your happiness unless you give it the authority to. Just like that, you can make yourself happy. With enough practice at being mindful, you can concentrate on anything with your full attention and focus. Your mind is the most powerful weapon you have in changing your mood!

How Can Mindfulness Make You Happy?

The sunlight doesn't set anything on fire on its own, but with the help of a magnifying glass, it quickly burns a piece of paper.

You can apply this same concept in your life when practicing mindfulness. Anything can be the object of your happiness -- different people feel happiness in different ways. Some feel happiest with their family, while others feel best surrounded by nature. It's up to you! If your family is your priority, remember to tell them that you love them and care for them, since their happiness will feed yours.

When you keep your mind from wandering into the worries of the past and the fears of the future, you can reach happiness through attention to the present. If you don't focus on the time you're spending with your source of happiness, mindfulness will elude you and you'll still be distracted. Facing your fears and fighting them with courage allows you to succeed in becoming a happier person.

How to be Present

To become a happy person, you need to be mindful and live in the present. It's not impossible to be present in the moment, but it's certainly difficult at first! Remember that you can enjoy anything in your life if you want to – it's all a state of mind.

Mindfulness comes about when you overcome your problems and realize that they don't really matter. What matters most is your present, not your past or your future. You only exists in the present, and if you miss the current moment, it will become a memory.

Happiness comes about from mindfulness, and both of them can transform your life. You can only become satisfied with your life and your assets when you stop judging yourself and others. The more you compare your successes with those of other people, the more stressed out and sad you'll become.

Do you want to be happy or sad? If you want to be happy, why do you dwell on things you can't change? When your colleague or your boss is giving you a hard time, and you're constantly thinking about how to deal with the situation, you can never become happy. Try your best and leave the rest!

Stop judging yourself. Focus on a cup of tea at your office, or the birthday of a friend. If you lose your job, this is stressful, but thinking about the ways to fix the problem rather than focusing on why you were fired is a more productive route to happiness. Don't pity yourself; there are many people who are in far worse shape than you. Focus on being happy for the life you have and the many advantages you enjoy. Jobs will come and go, but the time you waste worrying will never come back. You are given this life to be happy, to help others, and to live a life with purpose.

Reducing Stress using Mindfulness

You may have heard that self-reliance is more important that any medicine in this world for your well-being. Nowadays, people turn to psychiatrists for their worries, and take medications that affect their hormones. What is the benefit of these artificial ways to become happy? You might be damaging your body and brain with these drugs.

If you're constantly stressed and worrying about your marriage, your kids, your finances, and future insecurities, you're damaging yourself and your mind. Although it has no visible effects, stress is a very dangerous problem that can affect everything related to you. Your health, your body, your relationships, and your work life can suffer if you succumb to stress.

Stress can make you ill, both mentally and physically, and can drain away the joys of life. It's spreading like an epidemic these days, and people don't even notice when they become stressed out. Mindfulness can be the cure to your stress and worries if you use it in the right way. It's more powerful than painkillers and more effective than any doctor.

If you apply mindfulness in search of happiness, meditate, help others, and try to stop worrying, you can fight against stress every time it attacks you. Maintain both inner and outer balances to keep your fight-or-flight responses at an average level. There's no doubt that modern life is very difficult, and a lot of factors contribute toward having a stressful life, but you can't take this as an excuse for being unhappy.

Mindfulness can help you manage stress in many ways, by helping you improve your focus on happiness, improve your health, and become a happier person. You don't want to let stress take your happiness and enthusiasm for enjoying life away or lose the battle and succumb to sadness. Don't you want to remember this time in a positive way? If so, then start the practice of being mindful right now. It's possible anywhere and ay time -- while working in your office, while studying in your college, and while dealing with your children.

If your kids are stressing you out and you're responding by being angry, they will learn to react the same way. Teach them mindfulness by being present in the moment. The purpose of mindfulness is to make you stronger and braver, so that you can combat stress in your life with a positive perspective. If your boss is angry, maybe they're having a bad day at home, or maybe they've recently suffered the loss of someone close.

In this busy life, people think that watching television or checking your social media account can make you forget your worries. But social media itself is a cause of stress for many people, since they follow the lives of people they know who are rich and successful. These people didn't become rich in a moment -- they had bad times just like you, and they had to fight with stress too! Maybe they used mindfulness to focus on hard work and achieve the position they have now.

You'll be relieved to know that adding some time to practice mindfulness into your routine is not impossible, or even very hard. No specialized or expensive equipment is necessary for this, just the time to focus, and a commitment to reduce your stress and become a happier person. Resolve to start your meditation and practice today! If you work hard to think positively and be mindful, you'll find you can reduce your stress to more manageable levels.

Necessity is the mother of invention; similarly, mindfulness originated to treat stress and to promote self-healing. If you allow stress to take control of your life, you will find yourself going down a path to sadness, depression, and anxiety. But if you decide to fight it, you will become a better person with focused goals and a happier perspective.

Chapter 5: The Benefits Of Mindful Meditation

One of the first things that you notice when you practice mindful meditation on a regular basis is that your stress levels go down. You are able to look at situations that arise in a much more open manner. You don't let personal emotions get in the way of your thought processes. Of course, you still have emotions, but you are much more in control of them.

There are several health benefits to mindfulness that you may want to explore. This chapter will help you appreciate that mindfulness meditation may just be a good way forward in your life, if you want to live a more fulfilling and happy life, as well as not having to worry too much about the state of your health.

Blood pressure – During mindfulness meditation, your blood pressure goes down and your heart rate diminishes to a relaxed level. You are therefore able to calm yourself down in a way that is lasting.

Breathing – You learn to breathe in a specific way and be conscious of your breathing and thus are less likely to suffer from panic attacks – which are caused when you over oxygenate.

Anxiety and Depression – Mindfulness helps you to heighten your awareness so you are less likely to suffer from anxiety and depression.

<u>Metabolic Syndrome</u> – This accounts for high blood pressure, but it's also about the levels of cholesterol and triglycerides in your bloodstream. Studies have shown that people who practice mindfulness meditation are less prone to problems in this area.

<u>IBS and gut problems</u> – There has been a connection between mindfulness meditation and the improvement of gut problems. Perhaps this is brought about by awareness and less emphasis being placed upon incorrect eating habits.

<u>Cancer</u> – A significant study showed that patients who were mindful were better able to cope with cancer treatment and symptoms.

If you put aside the above health improvements that can be expected from mindful meditation, there are so many other improvements that people see within their lives when taking up mindfulness.

People are less prone to take time off from work. They are able to cope better with anger management. The other thing that is noticeable is that people are able to have better control over their emotional response to events that happen during the course of their lifetimes, because their approach is different.

Katy was always ill. She seemed to visit the doctor on a regular basis feeling like she had something very wrong with her. She believed that. The doctor had fobbed her off with medication for various ailments over the course of five years and when she started to make mindfulness a part of her everyday life, she suddenly realized where the problems were coming from. Instead of being able to face up to her self-esteem issues, she was using her health to justify her negative responses to life. As soon as mindfulness helped to take away those negative responses, she no longer felt the need to go to the doctor every five minutes.

Ian, on the other hand, was always worried about life. If he didn't have something to worry about, he would invent something. Mindfulness helped him to slow down his responses to everyday situations and stop using only the left hand side of the brain. He didn't see that there could be creative answers to his problems until he started to practice mindfulness meditation. It allowed him to stop his thought processes in their tracks and begin to see solutions in his life, thus eliminating his permanent sense of stress. Looking back on his life before mindfulness, Ian admits that he felt he was on his way to a nervous breakdown, but that he now understood that the negativity he was introducing into his life was of his own making. By adjusting his approach to life, he was now able to live a very happy and fulfilling lifestyle.

We have only mentioned the obvious health benefits of mindfulness but you may find, in your particular case, that mindfulness meditation helps you to focus on the "now" and enjoy life to its fullest without perpetually seeking solutions for things that have passed and that can never be changed. Much of the physical illness that humans suffer from arises from the approach that people have to life. For example, people who approach life with negativity are more likely to feel negative about their lives. What you learn through mindfulness is to take a more sensible approach to your life that adds to it, rather than detracts from it. The health benefits of your change of approach are very individual but definitely measurable.

Chapter 6: Secrets Of Flow

It is not uncommon for authors, artists, and musicians, alike, from time to time, to experience being in the flow state. Obviously, they excel and perform best in their art form when they are at their best. However, though it is common and easy to examine when creative people attain the flow state, they are not the privileged few for only whom the flow state is attainable.

Many of us have done well in our areas of expertise when we are in the flow as well. Perhaps, it might be our own inexperience with the flow that we may simply not have recognized it as well. Or perhaps it is because our fields may not be as creative as the arts that our state of flow might not have been easily recognizable, unlike the arts which itself is about self-expression.

In order to achieve a state of flow, flow theory postulates that three conditions have to be met. The first condition is that there must be a performer performing an activity with goals. For example, a singer must be singing a particular song. [4]

The second condition is that there must be a clear and immediate feedback. This can come from within the performer herself. As the singer sings, she can understand how well she is performing herself. Is she hitting all the correct notes? Is she enunciating her words accurately? Is the pitch correct? These are all questions she can answer as she is singing. This level of feedback is easiest to see through video games, which give you immediate feedback through a scoring system on the screen.

The last condition is that there must be a balance between the challenge of the performance and the skill level of the performer. The skill must be challenging enough for the performer to be engaged and challenged. It should neither be too easy that the performer becomes bored nor too difficult for the performer to achieve that the performer becomes discouraged.

Meanwhile, Schaffer proposed seven flow conditions:

Understanding what you are supposed to do

Getting an understanding of how to do it

Understanding how good you are executing it

Getting to know the place to go

Highly recognized challenges

The expertise that is highly perceived

Being free of distractions

So how do these seven conditions affect a performer achieving the state of flow? Imagine that you are an artist, who has found himself in the state of mindfulness. You are fully aware of your intention and that is to paint scenery of a sunset using oil paint on a canvas. Your goal is clear, meeting the first condition as proposed by Schaffer of getting to know what to do.

You have the skill set needed to complete an adequate painting, meeting the second condition of knowing how to do. You know that you have the skill set necessary to paint this particular painting and the success rate of you completing said painting is high. This lets you meet the third condition of knowing how well you are doing.

You are sure of the style of painting and the picture composition, thus letting you meet the fourth condition of knowing where to go. Though painting the scenery is challenging, you are confident of your skill to do so, meeting the fifth condition of having high perceived challenges. This refers to how the performer perceives the challenges that he or she will face in completing the goal.

The painting also requires you to have a high level of technique, which, again, may be challenging to you, and meets the sixth condition of high perceived skills. Like the perceived challenges, it is the perception of the performer that is important here. Does the performer think he or she has the skills required to complete the task? That is the imperative question. Whether he or she actually has the skills required is another question entirely.

The final condition of having freedom from distraction is met when and if you are painting in an environment that allows you to be fully focused on and is conducive to painting. This might require ample lighting, room to set up your easel and paints, and so forth.

Once the seven factors encompassing the state of the flow have been fulfilled, the most likely outcome is that the mind will have the optimal experiences in the flow.

People who experience the flow often describe it as being carried in the water current. Athletes often describe being in the state of flow as "being in the zone." One philosopher recall being in the state of flow during an invigorating conversation; while in the state of flow, he doesn't necessarily fathom he is experiencing flow. However, later he recognizes missing being in the state of flow after the conversation is over.[5]

Some religious mystics refer to achieving the flow as achieving nirvana or euphoria.[6]

Achieving the state of flow has many benefits. When you are in the flow, learning becomes effortless, because you are intrinsically motivated and self-directed. You take charge of your learning at your own pace.

The flow experience indicates a growth in mindset; you are responsible for your own actions. Since you must constantly challenge yourself to maintain the flow state, it helps stretch your skill level by motivating yourself to constantly seek growth. This, in turn, helps you master your skills.

Research also indicates that being in a state of flow increases performance in a wide variety of activities, including teaching, learning, and athletics.[7] Because there are personal growth and competency through the state of flow, your self-esteem also increases.

Reaching the state of flow also has a positive impact on overall life satisfaction. Various studies have shown the flow experience having a positive effect on people's lives. Since the flow experience is known to generate intense satisfaction and feelings of joy, it leads to happiness in the long run.

The personal growth and development achieved through flow also add to the intrinsic values we place on ourselves.

Since we can achieve higher mastery over skills through flow, we gain confidence in knowing our skills are above that of the average individual.

Mindfulness Exercise #4: Touching

For this exercise, you will need a tumbled stone or rock crystal. As many people resonate with the unique vibrations released by natural stones and crystals, it is always wise to use them in mindfulness exercises.

Follow the directions from the breathing exercise to get into the state of mindfulness.

Once you get into a rhythm with your breathing, gently hold the stone in your left hand and direct your attention to your palm and fingers. Feel the vibration or tingling sensation on your palm and fingers.

You can do this exercise anywhere you want. Simply carry the crystal with you in a bag or in your pocket.

Crystals are generally thought to have a multitude of benefits. Many people use crystals to improve their well-being through crystal healing. More information on this subject can be found by researching crystal healing.

However, their benefits will not be covered in this guide, as our primary objective is to practice being mindful of our touch as we continue to achieve mindfulness in our daily life.

Mindfulness Exercise #5: Drawing

While it can be argued that drawing is an innate skill, to draw well, you need to practice. Drawing is a great exercise that will facilitate the connection between our mind, eye, and hand. The best way to experience mindfulness is to draw from observation.

While in art school, students often learn the "continuous line drawing," a technique where you draw your observations without lifting the pen from the paper.

Because our main objective is to experience mindfulness, we will not be bothered with proportions or realistic nature of our drawings. Rather, we will focus on the activity of drawing itself.

For this activity, use a pen rather than a pencil. You will also need a blank piece of paper.

Find yourself a still life object - such as a vase or a bowl of fruits - as the subject of your drawing. Observe the subject in your chosen environment. Decide on a starting point. It could be the bottom of the vase or the top. It simply does not matter. Choose a starting point that you are comfortable with.

As you draw, pay close attention to your eye and your hand.

Feel the grip of your hand on the pen. Are you gripping too hard too loose? Adjust your grip and strength accordingly.

Next, examine if your eye and hand are in coordination. Is your pen drawing what you are seeing with your eye? Focus on moving your hand according to your eye.

Using these techniques, practice drawing five subjects you can find in your home.

Chapter 7: Improving General Health

Anyone who has ever practiced mindfulness can attest to its emotional benefits that have transformed their lives. Mindfulness is a way of life that brings about success in both a personal and professional capacity. Aside from the emotional benefits, mindfulness is critical in promoting physical health too. The following are some of the ways that mindfulness improves the general health of an individual.

Protects a person from falling sick and minimizes symptoms

The immune system is made up of a complex network of cells that fights away disease-causing agents. If you have a weak immune system, you become susceptible to all manner of diseases, your body becomes overwhelmed and it could be fatal. Scientific research has shown that mindfulness leads to a stabilized immune system by virtue of promoting healthy body cells. If the body cells are replenished and have sufficient energy, they are in a much better position to fight off disease-causing organisms.

Mindfulness also improves a person's ability to make better decisions. You never know where your illness could stem from, but for the most part, it's thanks to our ignorance and poor decisions. Mindfulness teaches us to be more observant and adopt healthy habits. For instance, if we have been indulging into foods prepared in unhealthy conditions, we start paying more attention to these foods, become aware of the risk we subject ourselves to, and ultimately, stop ourselves from ever eating these foods again. Thus, we protect ourselves against a potential illness.

Mindfulness not only allows us to drop the poor decisions that we have made but also empowers us to cultivate positive habits. At the end of the day, we are the result of our habits. If we have terrible habits, we suffer the consequences of which getting ill may be one of them, and if we have great habits, we become geared up for success. One of the positive habits that we can adopt is working out. While previously you would have gone to a bar during your free time, now you start attending the gym and as a result, your health is given a tremendous boost.

Mindfulness has been shown to promote the growth of the hormone that is critical in fighting off cancer cells. Mindfulness boosts the production of these hormones, thus empowering the body to protect itself against cancer. Additionally, mindfulness helps lessen the effects of cancer by promoting stress-reduction. A cancer victim is susceptible to being stressed out and this amplifies the cancer symptoms.

Mindfulness also helps HIV victims to deal with their condition by increasing the capacity of their body to defend itself. Mindfulness allows people to enjoy their lives despite the illnesses they may be struggling with.

Inflammation

When a part of your body suffers inflammation, it can be terribly distressing. It forbids you from having a normal life. But thanks to mindfulness, you can overcome inflammation. Mindfulness promotes brain health, thus making the brain more capable of mitigating the triggers for inflammation.

Mitigates eating disorders

Emotional eating is one of the problems that most people struggle with. Whenever they experience a slightly uncomfortable situation, the answer is reaching for a calorie-packed burger. And this has led them to become overweight. Mindfulness helps such people learn how to brave through uncomfortable situations without turning to food. It helps them to select carefully what they are going to eat and pay full attention to the process of eating. When one is fully focused during their meals, they are less likely to overeat. Mindfulness helps cultivate a great body image, thus encourages people to be happy with how they look and not fall into disorders like bulimia.

Weight loss

Most sweet-tasting foods tend to be calorie-laden. When we develop a habit of indulging in these sweet foods, for instance, junk foods and fail to mitigate the damage through workouts, ultimately we become obese. And with obesity, we are ushered into a phase of negative body image and other self-esteem issues. Mindfulness helps us to cultivate a healthy eating pattern. We become more interested in foods that nourish us as opposed to foods that are detrimental to our health. We start appreciating fruits and vegetables a lot more.

Helps us fight loneliness

The impact of loneliness can spread through everything that we touch. It will show in our work, in our mannerisms, and in our attitudes. Loneliness makes us less productive. The idea that you can only be lonely when you're secluded from people is erroneous. Mindfulness teaches us to always be full to the brim with positive energy so that negativity doesn't get a chance to sneak up on you. In this way, you could be alone but feel much fulfilled and at peace with both yourself and the universe. When you cease to needlessly feel lonely, you will improve the quality of your life.

Enhances brain performance

The brain is to the body what the CPU is to the desktop. It controls everything. If your brain is in a poor condition, this could hamper the proper functioning of your body. For instance, if you consume some harmful substance, it may affect your capacity to remember stuff or make proper decisions, thus lowering the quality of your life. Mindfulness enables you to improve your mental health and by proxy, your overall health.

Lowers risk of heart attack

Mindfulness has been shown to lower the risk of developing a heart attack. This comes about as the cumulative result of proper diet, exercising, meditation, health checkups, and improved relationships. Mindfulness promotes all the habits that are critical in the proper functioning of an individual at both the mental and emotional capacity. Thus, an individual who practices mindfulness has a lower risk of developing a heart attack.

Chapter 8: Benefits Of Mindfulness

With mindfulness, your physical & mental health can both be improved. What are you waiting for? Start including and practicing mindfulness techniques in your day-to-day activities every single day! Mindfulness techniques only require your acceptance and concentration. Without coming to any decision, you just need to pay attention to the thoughts, worries, fears & sensations purposely.

It takes plenty of time and practice to understand mindfulness techniques and, as any technique, practice makes perfect. As a beginner, if one technique is not working for you, then skip it and try another one on that resonates more to you..

Mindfulness improves your general well-being:

A lot of individuals who are in a habit of practicing mindfulness techniques can form deep and better connections with others and have no regrets about things that have happened in the past.

People practicing mindfulness techniques won't run from the situations they are afraid of. They will whole heartedly engage in activities and deal with adverse events if they happen.

Meditation can help your brain to function in a better way. It improves grey matter in areas linked with self-control & attention as it does in empathy, and self-awareness. It also calms the brain parts that create stress hormones and build around those areas that lift mood & encourage learning.

Mindfulness and Meditation both contribute to improving the control of sugar in your blood and aid towards helping sugar type 2 diabetes presence. Meditation lowers the risk of hypertension as well as helps reduce high blood pressure levels and improves heart & circulatory health.

Mindfulness very importantly also reduces self-destructive and addictive behavior. These include excessive alcohol intake and the abuse of illegal & prescribed drugs.

Mindfulness helps boost your overall physical health:

You will inevitably sleep much better as you won't have those constant nagging thoughts that worry you throughout the night

It helps relieve stress and tension promoting better muscular health

It lowers your blood pressure level

You will also achieve better results related to gastrointestinal difficulties & chronic pain which many times are associated to your level of stress and anxiety.

Mindfulness can help contribute towards the healing of:

Eating disorders

Obsessive-compulsive disorder

Couples' conflicts

Substance abuse

Anxiety disorders

Depression

Chapter 9: Putting Words Into Power And Perspective

From time to time we find ourselves tied by small issues that eventually leave us stressed and those minor things tend to occupy our brain. These little issues make us perform poorly in our tasks. Most of the time, we find that our brain is in constant worry of an issue that we take less time to suffer from. This worry is the problem itself but not what we are worrying about. One of these small but stressing issues includes our job. According to a study conducted by major companies, employees were diagnosed with some condition that resulted in the state of their work. Those who were not employed and had a better job showed better results.

An awkward situation makes you keep thinking of it even when you are not working on that situation. As we have mentioned above job can be stressing. This is why we find ourselves thinking about it even when we are not working; even during off. This limits your mental capability to think about the other things.

Placing thing into perspective is the best way to keep what you think and what you do to be relevant both to you and to those around you. It will help other individuals understand you and thus have a better interaction. Here are some ways that can help you attain this;

Learn to switch between activities – as we have learned in the meditation session; you should train yourself to be in the state of handling one task at a time. Once a task arises, use all your potential and effort to accomplishing that particular task. After it is done, you should learn how to switch quickly to the next task at hand. This will leave you with less room to strain your brain. An example is if you happen to get out of a job, you should leave everything behind and focus on having a great time with your family.

Learn to deal with frustrations – from time to time we get frustrated, and a disappointment leaves us stressed and downed toe earth. This should not be the case we should learn how to deal with frustration as fast and smoothly as possible. Rehashing our frustration will only make the situation worse than it was initially, instead, have a moment to meditate on the issue and leave room for your mind to relax through mindfulness, this will make the mind and body, as well as your emotion, learn to move on the past that frustration. Sleep - giving your body time to sleep will make sure that it gets time to refresh and be ready for the next day activity. Lack of sleep has been associated with conditions such as depression and stress as well as ADHD. Eight hours of sleep a day will work and a nap in between work hours will reduce the stress hormones and boost the immune system making you perform better.

Be mobile – the perspective that you view exercise in determine how healthy you doing regular activities will ensure that you get the maximum flexibility your body need to be fit. Exercise will help your body burn excess calories and make your organs perform optimally. Exercises have also been connected to reduced anxiety. The exercise should not be that extensive, a few walk in the park can be the best way to start. You can also walk home instead of driving.

Take a moment alone - having a moment away from distraction will make you have a time for you own self. This is the time that you will get to reflect on your health and your mind. This can be the best time to meditate or have a yoga practice. This will rejuvenate you and make you have a new start as well as help you face a stressful event.

Socialize with others- socializing has been proved to be a good way to curb stress and depression, in case you are undergoing a difficult time, you may find it helpful to share with friends and family members. By doing so, you will be relieved of your burden, and this will ensure that you are emotionally and mentally fit.

The way you view things (perspective) will determine the way you handle problems. You must learn how to see a thing in a positive outlook so that it will be easier to adapt. If for example you are faced with a difficulty, you need to train your mind to have an active mind and set and believe that you can overcome the situation.

Perspective makes a difficult situation easy to solve. Motivation will come in handy to make you have a better perspective on life. You also need to have high ability to put words into power. Words can be powerful if used in the right way; you should learn to accomplish what you plan and what you say. You must be in the capacity to make everything work. Make everything work.

Chapter 10: Mindfulness Exercises Through Relaxation And Efforts.

Mindfulness through effort simply means, doing what you have to do. While some people do possess lots of energy, and they are always on the move, in search of what to do, others will require some "push" or assistance, just to get going. In meditation, you just don't seek what to do, rather, just to escape, rather you are developing some efforts internally. It means observing your mind and then concentrating on a subject matter.

There is a believe that putting too much effort will make you restless, and putting too little effort will make you dull. In mindfulness, the state of your body and the mind are definitely a measure of your effort. If you are unsure about how to start a mindfulness exercise for relaxation and effort, have a stand on your feet, then align your body by pulling out your chest and then make your spine straight.

#1: The sitting posture

This is perhaps the commonest mindfulness posture exercise you need to learn. When done repeatedly, the sitting posture exercise will definitely improve your overall posture and thus boosting your feeling of confidence.

Step #1: Sit uprightly on a chair with your feet on the ground and your back rested on the seat.

Step #2: Allow your legs to be separated.

Step #3: Make sure your torso is located at right angle to your thigh.

Step #4: close your mouth and eyes in order to rest them during this exercise, and don't try to force a smile, rather allow your mouth to take its natural shape.

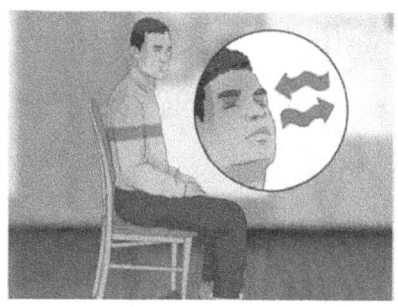

#2: The standing posture

The standing posture is a mindfulness posture that you can practice at any time of the day. The standing posture is also important because it is the foundation for many other postures, likewise, it will promote your overall wellbeing and confidence.

Step #1: stand upright and let your feet to remain parallel and must be separated by shoulder width.

Step #2: slightly allow your knees to bend.

Step#3: Gently raise your arms to a level where your hands become even or slightly lowered below your shoulders.

Step #4: allow your elbows to bend slightly.

Step #5: Let your hands remain at one-foot length apart, while your palms are pointing downwards.

Step #6: Let your fingers slightly curved and separated, while pretending that you are holding a ball in your hand in a relaxed way.

Step #7: Just like you did in the sitting posture, allow your eyes and mouth to remain closed in an unforced natural way.

Step #8: Remain in this position for about 5 minutes and then relax for about 15 seconds before repeating the position. You can perform between 3 and 5 repetitions at a time.

#3 The walking posture

You can practice the walking posture in your spare time, and it is a posture that will help you remain relaxed even when you are walking. Keep in mind that the walking posture will require a larger practice space than the sitting posture, hence you must plan accordingly.

Step #1: Make sure your foot is lifted with your heel first.

Step #2: Take a step forward with your left foot first.

Step #3: Let your body and hands sway in the right way while you move.

Step #4: Only step your right food forward after your left has been completely placed on the ground.

Step#5: You can repeat this step for about 25 minutes or longer.

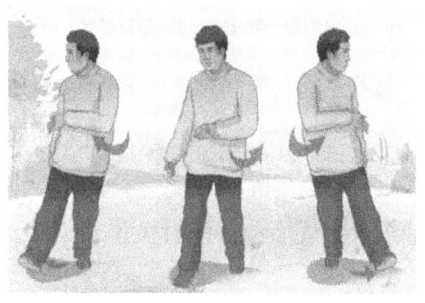

#4: Other basic postures

There are several other postures you can try out aside the sitting, standing and walking postures in mindfulness. Always keep in mind that the different postures you practice will focus on different parts of the body, likewise you can use them to hone diverse mental techniques that can promote your spiritual awareness. Do not forget that all these techniques will demand your previous breathing, mental, and relaxation skills.

- The Supine posture- This posture requires that you lay down. Make sure you lay on your back while allowing your legs to stay straight, with your arms staying straight by your side. This is one of the postures intended to enhance body relaxation.

- The sideways lying - To perform this posture, simply lay on your side, while keeping the upper body straight. Make sure your legs are bent slightly, and then place the upper hand gently on your hip while your lower hand is placed by the head. This posture practice is intended to relax your body and mind.

- The Half Lotus posture- To practice this posture, you will have to sit up while you allow your left foot to rest on your right thigh (this should be under the left knee), and make sure your hands are rested on your knees. This posture will help stretch your lower body and legs.

- The cross-legged posture – You need to sit upright to perform this posture. Cross your legs, while resting your hands in front of your stomach. This posture will help in stretching your legs and you will become relaxed.

Chapter 11: Incorporating Mindfulness In Other Routine Activities

As I mentioned earlier, to become mindful at all times, you have to incorporate mindfulness into as many of your everyday activities to train your mind to stay focused on the task that you are currently doing.

Here is a list of activities that you can do mindfully to incorporate mindfulness in your life.

Mindful Showering

You may have noticed that whenever you shower, either you think of the activities you have done throughout the day or you plan for the activities that you need to do in that day.

This is not particularly helpful while training your mind to become mindful, as you are not focusing on the task that you are currently doing, which is why you need to shower mindfully in order to stay mindful at all times.

Here is how you can do that:

While you are taking a shower, make sure that you focus on your body and how the water falling on your body makes you feel when it touches certain parts of your body. When water droplets fall on the back of your neck, feel how it releases the pressure in your body making you feel relaxed.

Feel the droplets of water hitting your body and changing your body's temperature. For instance, if you are taking a cold shower, notice how each droplet releases the heat from your body, as it touches your body.

Feel water trickling on different parts of your body; your head and the wetness of your hair while showering, the feeling of water on your eyes, face, nose mouth, chin etc., your neck, your chest, your back, your belly, your butt, your sex organs all the way down to your toes. Feel how the shoes feel while you are taking a shower.

How the soap feels on your hand and literally everything involved in taking a shower; feel it and notice it without judging it.

Make it a habit to shower this way every time so you can train your mind to stay focused on the activity you are currently doing.

Mindful Walking

Walking is another activity we all do carelessly without paying attention to it. Do you remember any walk wherein you concentrated on walk itself rather than paying attention to the thoughts popping in your head e.g. where you are going (the future), how you might be late (future), your previous experiences while going to the same place (if applicable), how it is your first time, whether you look good enough to impress etc.

Your answer to whether you are ever mindful when walking will most probably be a big 'No'. That's right. Nobody pays attention to walking itself, as it comes natural to us.

For this reason, it's a great activity to train your mind to stay mindful of at all times.

Here is how you can walk mindfully.

Whenever you walk, pay attention to your feet. Notice how your feet feel when you lift them up from the ground and then place them back while you're taking steps.

Feel the joints moving in your body as you walk, feel how your knee caps move while you try to lift your foot and also pay attention to the muscles as they expand or contract to make possible for your legs and feet to move.

Observe your form, starting from your head, down to your neck, abdomen, back, legs, hands etc. Just notice how you are walking and envision yourself as a whole; as if you are a third party looking from a distance. Just notice and let what you see pass. Notice every single part of the walking including how your clothes feel as you walk, the feel of air hitting various parts of your body while you are walking etc.; there is just a lot to notice so notice everything if you want to be fully mindful of your walking.

Make a habit to walk this way by paying attention to the movement rather than getting lost in your thoughts. Doing this on a regular basis helps you stay mindful of yourself and your surroundings at all times.

Mindful Brushing

Another great activity to train your mind to stay mindful at all times is brushing. As brushing your teeth is something you do on regular basis, doing it mindfully will help you stay focused on the other activities you do throughout the day. Here is how you can brush mindfully.

Rub the brush against your teeth slowly so you can notice the parts of your mouth that are being cleaned by the brush. Feel the bristles moving back and forth against your teeth making them clean and getting rid of the plague on them.

Pay attention to the taste of toothpaste on your tongue and in your mouth so you can distract your mind from getting lost in thoughts. Pay attention to each tooth, as you rub it with your toothbrush. When you gargle after you have brushed your teeth, rinse your mouth with water and feel how the water feels inside your mouth.

These are just ideas; there are many sensations, feelings and encounters you have while brushing teeth including the positioning of your hand on the mouth, how you hold the brush, where the toothpaste is placed on the toothbrush and much more- the options are limitless so make sure to experience as many of these opportunities as possible.

Practice mindful brushing this way and soon, you will start to notice that you are becoming more mindful on other aspects of your life, as you will observe that you only focus on the activities you do.

In addition, slowly bring mindfulness in each and everything you do. From doing laundry to cooking a meal to doing a task at workplace- do everything mindfully to always stay conscious of your thoughts so you live in the present and keep stressful thoughts and ideas away.

In addition to doing the practices discussed above, you can cultivate mindfulness in your routine by focusing on two important activities that you do in your daily routine: listening and observation. You spend most of your day doing these two activities yet you don't pay any attention to them. As a result, you feel stressed as your mind is lost in thoughts of the past or future which brings you stress or anxiety. However, if you train your mind to do these two activities mindfully, you can become mindful of yourself all the time and increase your level of awareness.

Here's how you can practice mindful listening and observation.

Mindful Listening

When you hear a sound or voice that is recognizable, you make a preconception of the person speaking based on the past experience with him/her. Often, you don't actually listen to that person mindfully and don't pay attention to what he/she is saying.

For instance, if a colleague at work you don't like much advises you to make your project report a certain way, it is likely you'll feel he is giving you bad advice and won't listen to him mindfully.

This practice isn't a healthy one because when you focus on the presumptions you have created, you get lost in your own unhealthy thoughts, which makes you feel stressed. This also affects your relationship with that person and never lets you form an unbiased image of him.

Mindful listening is an exercise designed to listen to sounds, voices, music and everything in a non-judgmental way. By practicing this exercise, you train your mind to stay neutral to any sound and perceive each sound in an unbiased manner.

Here is how you can practice mindful listening.

How to Practice Mindful Listening

Select something that you have never heard before and play it; it could be a piece of music from your own collection or you can turn the radio dial until you come across something that you haven't heard before.

Put on your headphones and close your eyes. Try not to judge the artist's name or genre of the music; instead, just listen to it neutrally and allow yourself to get lost in the melody and lyrics until the track ends.

Don't change it if you dislike the melody at first as the sole reason of this practice is not to develop a preconception. Listen till the end and try to involve yourself in the beats.

Do it on daily basis and soon you will make it a habit to listen mindfully to everything.

Mindful Observation

Mindful observation is another great strategy to stay mindful at all times as this is another activity you do mindlessly most of your day.

Mindful observation is an incredibly powerful exercise which is designed to increase your mindfulness while observing things. You can practice mindful observation by paying attention to the beauty nature has to offer or anything around you to be consciously aware of things you see in your routine.

This helps you perceive things for what they are instead of being judgmental.

How to Practice Mindful Observation

Here is how you can practice mindful observation.

Choose a natural object from the environment you are currently in and focus on it. It could be an insect, a flower, the moon or clouds; whatever you can see in your immediate environment. Look at it with the curiosity of a child, as if you've never seen it before. Analyze every bit of it; its shape, formations, texture, size, where it is placed, immediate environment, color etc.

Notice the beauty of the object you are observing and pay close attention to it. Explore its formation visually and don't think of anything else while you are observing it. You'll soon become engrossed in it and will start to appreciate it.

Do this for 10 minutes twice daily and slowly incorporate mindful observation all the time so you cultivate a habit of it.

To improve your state of mindfulness and also to keep track of your progress, there is one more activity you should do on daily basis: mindful journaling.

Mindful Journaling

Mindful journaling is a great technique you can use to improve your state of mindfulness by keeping track of your progress on a daily basis. Here is how you can practice this:

Write a journal on daily basis by recording each activity that you have done mindfully on that day. For instance, if you have done mindful showering then record it on the journal.

Notice what problems you faced while doing activities mindfully and what solutions you came up with to resolve these problems. For instance, if you tried to eat mindfully and you had problems eating your meal slowly write it down. If you came up with a solution to eat with chopsticks rather than eating by a fork as it was difficult to grab food with chop sticks so you naturally ate slower then write it in your journal to acknowledge your efforts to be more mindful of yourself.

Notice the effects of doing an activity mindfully on your day. Did you stay mindful for an hour after the activity or did you just get lost in your thoughts as soon as you finished doing the activity? Record the time (estimate) you stayed mindful on your journal and write what made you get lost in your thoughts.

Come up with a solution to stay mindful for a longer period of time next day, record it in the journal and do it on the next day. Observe if your solution has worked for you or not and write that on the journal at the end of the day. If it has worked, keep doing it more the next day and if it didn't work then come up with another solution and do it.

Maintain your journal this way to record your progress and also to figure out what works for you and what doesn't. You will soon devise a custom strategy for yourself to stay mindful at all times.

In addition to doing this, staying mindful of the stress and tension in your body is important so you can manage that stress on time and feel relaxed and happy. The next chapter teaches you how to do that through body scan mindfulness meditation.

Chapter 12: Calm The Feelings

Our feelings are really beautiful, I think that's what makes us human. They give us passage to passion, pleasure, affection and laughter. Then, on the other hand, let us feel deep pain, sorrow, hate, and then terror. What is it that makes us superhuman?

Emotions play a pivotal role in activating those emotions that serve as a guide for us, respecting others and our environment, and knowing when we need to defend ourselves.

Nevertheless, living our lives through our emotions will take us on an emotional roller coaster that generates only negative, dramatic external responses. Not helping us to better interpret circumstances and experiences. An unreality of feeling.

Recognizing our feelings and tracking them back inside ourselves to their origins will help us understand why we respond unconsciously to certain individuals or circumstances. Bringing us precious spiritual insight as well. Allowing us to respond in a calm and peaceful manner. Providing approaches that are focused on consistency and intuitive understanding. Higher consciousness.

Instead of understanding the rage of pain, sorrow, grief, disappointment, and then concentrating on seeing nothing but the emotion itself. That's how we get stressed, tired, nervous, and very close.

I'm going to use Martial Arts as an example simply because I know the course. If faced with a violent confrontation, there may be physical harm. We must protect ourselves. When we allow our emotions to take over feeling fear it will paralyze the body, it will become paralyzed and unable to transfer fluid. It leaves you unable to protect yourself at all.

They must identify the triggering of the fear mechanism, then return to the calmness and consistency of one's normal emotional state. This is where the magic happens that your body is free and clear your mind and heighten your senses.

Allowing extraordinary reactions and a definite self-defense ability.

Our emotions used in this way give every aspect of our lives, strong intuition and perspective, allowing us the tranquility to respond positively and react to our environment and relationships without disrupting any internal balance for our highest good.

Everyone's got a peaceful, happy place inside, educated or not. We can become a spiritual warrior capable of helping others and ourselves with a simple switch of thinking (in turn feelings). Never allow your emotional state to be dictated by anyone else. You're in control of that.

Strategies to Help Control Your Emotions

You hear about strategies for growing a business, generating leads, and the like all the time, but what is it that Americans are dealing with more than anything else? The concentrating and manipulating the strength of their emotions.

The ability to concentrate the mind is important during a time of stress, as is the importance of learning how to control the emotions. But what if that talent isn't yours? What's the best way to make you feel comfortable? Especially if you're feeling sick, you're so scared of what could happen next.

The minds of most people move like a dragonfly, flitting every few seconds. Millions of people are suffering from anxiety, fear, depression, and so on, and suffering because they are giving away their attention. You may have paid prolonged attention to a particular object (TV, media, fears, lack of focus on positive things, etc.) creating multiple distractions within yourself and your emotions is the barometer from where your focus has gone.

Distractions disrupt the mind and don't like ambiguity. Confusion causes confusion, and emotionalism contributes to discomfort.

Have you ever tried to keep your mind quiet for a minute? It might sound offensive to say that, if you have the right tools to use, it's quite easy to quiet your mind. But there needs to be a willingness to take charge of where you concentrate.

Let me first show that you can take control of your mind, stay focused and learn how to control your emotions. But you have to do it consciously, no one can control your mind for you, not even your analyst.

What was today's worst thing you've heard? How do you feel when you're talking about it?

Just days away is April 15th, if your taxes are already being paid, with a refund on the way, how do you feel?

What was the funniest thing that happened at the reception on your best friend's wedding day?

Science has repeatedly proven that our neuropeptides are influenced by what we focus on, named by some of the Molecules of Emotions. So why are millions of people concentrating on the worst? Because teasing seems more fun than calmly taking some time to learn how to do something else. Nobody else does it, so why are we supposed to?

Because it gives you the real power to relax the mind. Doesn't take much work, and it can be incredibly rewarding. So, how are you doing this?

Stand in a safe place for 30-45 seconds to focus. Sit up straight and slowly and deeply breathe in. Exhale and repeat your intake 3 times.

Look at something right in front of you. Reflect on it for 10-12 seconds. How would you tell a blind person about it?

Now look directly above you at one thing. Reflect on it again for 10-12 seconds. How would you tell a blind person about this? It's very important the info.

Look down at last. Reflect on it again for 10-12 seconds. How would a blind person explain this? Focusing on the information is important.

Congratulations, you have controlled your mind and body successfully for the last 45 seconds (assuming you have done that brief exercise). All we need to do now is broaden your understanding of the actual control you have. You'll start noticing a change if you do this several times a day.

Next, take a deep breath, hold your breath for the count of 5, then breathe all the air in your lungs and hold for the count of 3. You start to take a deep breath every time you start to feel your emotions well. The breath is one of the best ways to cool the body. Motion= emotion and you have very little control when breathing high and shallow in your chest.

If that's something you'd like to learn more about, or you find this book interesting, let me know and I'm going to give you more ideas and techniques to master this topic.

Calm Emotions: How to Make Yourself Feel Centered and Serene

Calm my emotion and feel more relaxed. If that's something you've noticed, you're not alone. With the stress level that most people are in these days, it's all too easy for emotions to turn upside down.

Figuring out how to relax emotions and combat stress starts with knowing in the first place what triggers our emotional state. Although individual experiences and emotions influence emotional responses, they are also greatly affected by brain chemistry. If your brain chemistry's delicate balance is disturbed, it can lead to a variety of symptoms including mood swings, anxiety, and eating and sleeping issues.

To provide a foundation for good emotional wellbeing, it is necessary to ensure that the correct amount of neurotransmitters, hormones and other substances that affect brain function is preserved. So, you might think, by enhancing brain chemistry, how can I control my emotion? In reality, there are many ways to accomplish this, including healthy lifestyle choices and support from outside sources.

Your diet contains most of the nutrients you need, including your brain, to keep your entire body working properly. A balanced diet rich in vegetables, fruits and whole grains can help to calm emotions and avoid alcohol, smoking and narcotics, all of which can have a detrimental effect on brain chemistry.

Another response to how I can calm my emotion is to get rid of stress. In many health issues, stress is the number one culprit, not the least of which is anxiety and mood swings. Getting the right amount of sleep and using relaxation techniques such as sound and aromatherapy can go a long way to help relieve your life's added stress.

Such lifestyle choices, of course, may not be all you need to help calm your emotions. There are 100 per cent natural herbal remedies that can provide the brain with the neurotransmitters and hormones it needs to function properly to fill the gaps that your regular diet increasing leave. These therapies, based on centuries-old concepts of healing, help balance brain chemistry and manage emotional response.

You may be asking yourself how to relieve my anger with natural remedies. It's pretty simple. These remedies have been proven to help control mood swings, improve self-confidence and calm emotions by using a unique blend of herbs and plant-based ingredients such as St. John's Wort and Passion Flower. And they do not bear any serious side effects because they are completely natural.

Many of us fall into the trap of emotional upheaval, but with the calming power of nature, if you feel your emotions get away from you, you can get things back under control. Sleep well, get plenty of sleep and exercise and start using all-natural remedies to help keep the brain chemistry safe. You'll feel better in no time with a little natural boost.

Overcome Just This One Emotion to Cure Depression

Depression is mostly in the brain for many ignorant people. When they showed symptoms of anxiety disorder, parents ridiculed their kids for' creating drama.' Anxiety is a serious problem that needs to be understood and handled.

Biologically speaking, anxiety is a physiological, psychological, and behavioral state a body enters when it feels threatened— like a struggle— or a situation of flight. This hazard could be either real or future. The danger is potentially' in the brain' most of the time, but the body reacts to it as if it were physical. And, while the mind may think of any threatening situation that may never arise, the response of the body is the same as it would be in a threatening situation.

While anxiety is a state, it's fear that governs the emotion. Often the word fear is used in connection with anxiety, but it is also the basis on which anxiety is that.

So, is it anomalous and harmful to fear?

If asked to address a large group of people or deliver a study, most of us felt paralyzing fear. Or there were life-threatening situations where it would be odd to feel anything but fear. This fear is justified, but the fear that leads to anxiety is what.

Despite the same emotion, the threat is not real. You're afraid of things that either won't happen at all or it's distant from the odds. Not only that, it's not natural the compulsive fear that something could happen in an anxiety situation. And if you learn to deal with fear and calm your nerves when you're afraid, this will help to reduce anxiety through leaps and boundaries.

How is it possible to curb fear?

Think Positive Thoughts: It's easier to say than to do. When you're feeling anxious, it's because you're mostly thinking about negative thoughts that you're dwelling on anything that can go wrong. So how can you think of positive thoughts? You need to make a conscious effort to transform the brain from negative to positive.

Try to challenge the idea behind it when you are overwhelmed by this destructive fear-inducing thoughts. Anthony Robbins ' strategy is very useful. He explains how it will be weakened by challenging the belief behind negative thoughts in his book' Awaken the Giant Within.' And once weakened, replacing them with positive ones is simpler. So, for example, if you're concerned that if someone approaches your door with a knife in hand, question this reasoning by asking' just how can they do when the doors are locked' or' my parents are right next door.' When you begin to feel the negative thoughts are giving away, try to think about positive thoughts instantly.

Speak to someone you trust: Any kind of help feels heaven-sent when people are afraid. People with anxiety disorders have to learn to network and form a support group. Or you could just talk to a good friend. You don't have to deliberate about the cause of your fears or even the situation you're in, just talk normally and have a conversation to get your mind off all.

Calm yourself: If you're feeling the predominant emotion of fear, you're shooting heart rate and starting to feel dizzy. It may seem difficult to feel calm in this situation but to overcome anxiety, it needs to be replaced by a sense of calm.

The oldest trick in the book is deep breathing. You can also write down your worries in order to calm down. Exercising again works wonders, not only does some physical activity shift the focus of your brain, but also helps with anxiety and fear the chemicals released in your brain to exercise.

Tackle the root of the issue-This may help a select group of people, but once you identify the root of this fear, you'll be in a better position to address it. For some people, anxiety and fear are associated with a vivid childhood or adolescent memory. If you can trace the source back to an incident or environment that led to anxiety, tap it.

Only sit and try to focus on this incident in an isolated place. Try to connect with the younger you and try to help you feel comfortable in this situation with this younger version. This diminishes the incident's blow to your younger self and thus to the present. This takes time and you're going to have to make an effort to connect with the younger you, but it helps.

Fear is an emotion, and you cannot completely get rid of it like other emotions. You can only manage it, suppress it, not let it hang over you, and you can easily deal with anxiety and panic attacks as well once you do that.

Chapter 13: Practicing Meditation

Once you have decided on a posture that suits you it is time to relax into that posture and begin your meditation session.

Relax into Your Meditation Posture. You want to develop a sense of calm and focus during your meditation session. As a beginner it may take some time to settle down into your meditation. Take this time to examine the four foundations of mindfulness, what are the four frames of reference for you to study.

First Foundation, Mindfulness of the Body. With this you are making an examination of your body's composite nature, known as the body-mindfulness such as mentally noting, exploring, and focusing on component parts of your body such as hair, skin, head, teeth, heart, stomach, etc. This practice helps you to learn what they are, where they are, what they do, and what they are dependant on, etc.

• Focus on individual parts of your body and study them. These parts of your body may come to you as an image or in other ways.

• Make sure to also focus on the "in and out" breathing as this is also mindfulness of the body.

• Other aspects you may think about studying here are the liquid, solids, temperatures, and motion characteristics.

- Another aspect is the movement and how it interacts with different events in your life, muscle tension, tiredness, and other phenomena. Your body struggles against many different physical experiences daily, but without the mind it would be just an inactive lump of skin and bones.

Second Foundation Mindfulness of Physical Feelings and Sensations. This foundation of meditation is often known or referred to as "body-states" meditation to differentiate it from body-mindfulness.

- One thing to focus on is when and how sensations occur. Are they neutral, pleasant, or unpleasant? You can take a mental note that "there is pain here" or "there is a pleasant feeling here", etc.

Study and learn how your body is acting and interacting with these feelings.

• You can use a form of body scanning that can apply to the first two foundations, basically you scan your body up and down and examine sensations. You can watch this energy flow, allowing it to pass onto another part of your body.

• This skill will allow you to learn to deal with stress that arises, an how to relax and reduce tension. It will also give you insight and gain tolerance and understanding of your body's nature.

Third Foundation Mindfulness of Mental States. The third foundation covers dreams, ideas, fantasies, thoughts, and images. You need to learn how to focus and watch and learn how they arise, dependant on feelings, or outside influences or impulses, realize the amount of concentration you have. You can take mental notes on situations such as "all of a sudden this idea came to me", or "I no longer have that thought, it has changed into this." Here is where you can study the benefit or value of thoughts and themes.

• The other practice is to learn to let go of mental experiences, allow yourself to see them but not to get caught up in them or the practice will grind to a halt.

Fourth Foundation Mindfulness of the Consciousness. Mindful of the consciousness may include state of minds such as energetic states, tiredness, unfocused, focused, feeling peaceful, or anxious, etc.

• Does your mind want something or is it rejecting something? Is your mind dominated by feelings of anger or greed? These are questions to ask to help give you an awareness of what your mind's current thoughts are.

• The state of your consciousness can affect the themes of your fantasies and thoughts. If you are feeling tired, you may have feelings of depression. If you are feeling happy and energetic, this will make your mind feel happy and bright. If you have too many things going on in your head at once you won't be able to focus.

- The skill you need to learn is how to temper or gently change the state of your consciousness, so when you are feeling depressed, introduce compassion. When you have feelings of anger, introduce goodwill. Or feel appreciation when you feel dissatisfaction.

When Taking Note. When you are focusing you can take note of things verbally or mentally. To help build up your concentration you should try using a mental note. But if you feel more comfortable using verbal than use what is most comfortable for you. You want to gain insight on how your mind reacts to words and knowledge.

- Try and work towards having a silent awareness and eventually a word-less awareness where you are aware without using labels or words.

Chapter 14: Mindfulness With Food

Being mindful with food can help several areas of your life. Research SHOWS that thoroughly chewing your food improves digestion. Many of us in our busy lives multitask while we eat, whether it is having lunch at the desk, eating while watching television, or any other combination, we are often distracted and do not enjoy our food to the fullest or properly consume. When mindfulness is used with eating, it promotes a healthier relationship with food.

Food is meant to be savored, but when looking at a list of how to eat mindfully, it can be overwhelming. Choose one or two items and work on them until they come naturally, and then add in others. This is a technique to help become more mindful, not more stressed!

Close your eyes and smell your food. Take a deep breath in, noticing the different aspects of what you are smelling. Does it smell sweet or savory? Does the smell feel different when you first breath in versus in the back of your throat? Is it accompanied by a hot or cold sensation?

Think about the ingredients in the food. What route do you think they had to take to end up in front of you? Imagine where the ingredients came from and allow yourself to feel grateful to the people who facilitated the transportation.

Take a bite of food and chew it at least thirty times before swallowing. Notice the different flavors and textures as you roll it around on your tongue.

Don't eat in a place where it will be easy to get distracted from your food, such as: in front of the television, at your desk, or while using your phone.

Put your utensil down after every bite.

Take a moment to be grateful for the meal you are about to eat or have finished eating.

Stop and notice what reaction your body and emotions have to the food you are eating. Are you excited to be eating? In a hurry? Do you quickly put food into your mouth? Or are you a naturally slower eater?

By taking the time to be in the moment with your food, it can help facilitate gratefulness in your life for the food that you are able to eat and also help with portion control. The more we notice and pay attention to how we interact with food, the healthier our relationship with food will become.

Mindfulness as a Self-Check-Up

There are various techniques that can be used to check in with yourself to see how you are doing and even to help yourself through a situation, such as anxiety, sadness, and anger.

Techniques for Self-Check-Ups

These techniques can be used one after another or separately. Take time to practice at least one technique throughout the week while you are feeling good so that you can be in the habit to use it when you need a little check-in.

Body Scan

1) Find somewhere that you can sit upright and put your feet on the floor. Keep your body upright, but slightly relaxed.

2) Close your eyes and take in a deep breath.

3) Let go of any feelings from the day and focus on your breathing.

4) Once you've fallen into a pattern of noticing your breathing, feel your body in the chair and your feet on the floor.

5) Starting at the top of your head, start a systemic body scan. Very slowly move from the top of your head down. Do you feel any tightness or tension?

6) Keep moving your scan down your body to your ears, eyes, mouth. Scrunch up your face and release.

7) Move slowly to your neck and shoulders. Lean into any tightness, if you so choose.

8) Move your awareness on to your arms, elbows, hands, and then fingers.

9) Continue to make your way down your body, noticing what each part is feeling.

10) Once you've reached your toes, take a moment to notice your breathing again, sitting in your breath pattern.

11) Finally, return your awareness to any places in your body that you feel need more attention.

12) Take a moment to be grateful before opening your eyes and moving on for the day.

The body scan exercise generally takes about five to ten minutes and can be utilized throughout the day. Before a big meeting at work or in your car in the parking lot before an interview. It can be helpful in the morning to prepare you for the day. Find what works best for you.

Thought Observation

1) Find a comfortable place to be. Choose an amount of time for this exercise, generally between five to ten minutes, and set a timer so you will not be distracted by checking the clock.

2) Focus on your breathing.

3) Let your thoughts wander and notice where they go. Watch them float by like clouds in the sky, but don't latch on to them. If you do notice yourself flying away with a thought cloud, simply pull yourself back with no judgment.

4) When your time is over (if you want additional time, feel free to continue), take a moment to focus on your breathing again.

5) Finally, end your mindfulness exercise with a moment of gratitude for something in your life.

This exercise allows thoughts to flow freely by, and you may notice things that come up that you don't normally think about in the day-to-day because of busyness.

Morning Pages

1) Take a journal or other writing materials to a quiet place.

2) Take a few deep breaths and notice how you are feeling.

3) Writing three pages of stream-of-conscious in your journal. Don't edit what you are thinking or try to change it. Simply write what naturally comes to mind.

4) You can choose to either review everything you've pulled out of your head, or you can put your journal away, take a few deep breaths, and engage in the rest of your morning routine.

This is a common exercise in mindfulness. Take a few minutes out of your morning routine and it can help you get out of your head. The amount of time it will take depends entirely on you.

Mindfulness in the Mundane

Practicing mindfulness doesn't have to happen in large spaces of time. They can happen in the mundane and routine. This one, in particular, is about brushing your teeth, but consider what other areas in your life can you engage your senses and be mindful in the mundane.

While you are brushing your teeth, notice how the toothbrush feels in your hand. What does it feel like on your teeth? What is the flavor of your toothpaste? Let go of your thoughts about what you are going to do or what has happened today. Feel your feet grounding you to the floor, holding you up as you brush your teeth. Can you smell your toothpaste? Take a moment to reflect and be grateful for what brushing your teeth does for your health.

Mindfulness for Anxiety

While any mindfulness technique can be helpful to reduce anxiety, there are two listed below that specifically target anxious energy.

Loving-kindness

1) Sit or stand in a comfortable position and focus on your breathing.

2) Once you feel in rhythm with your breathing, say these traditional phrases to yourself:

May I be free from inner and outer harm and danger. May I be safe and protected.

May I be free of mental suffering or distress.

May I be happy.

May I be free of physical pain and suffering.

May I be healthy and strong.

May I be able to live in this world happily, peacefully, joyfully, with ease.

3) Next, think of someone that you love and who brings joy into your life.

4) Repeat the phrases above, replacing "I" with the name of the person you have chosen.

5) Think of someone whom you feel neutral about.

6) Repeat the phrases above, replacing "I" with the name of the person you have chosen.

7) Think of someone whom you feel difficult feelings toward.

8) Repeat the phrases above, replacing "I" with the name of the person you have chosen. If you are unable to do so, return

to the first person you sent loving-kindness and repeat to them. After you have done this, attempt to return to the person whom you have difficult feelings toward.

9) Finally, send loving-kindness to all beings by taking the phrases above and replacing "I" with "all beings."

10) Once this is completed, take a moment to notice how you feel. What emotions are you having? Do you notice any decreased or increased tension in your body?

11) End this exercise by taking a few deep breaths.

This mindfulness exercise is very unique in that we focus on something outside of our current environment.

Mindful Breathing

1) Find a comfortable place to be.

2) Sit tall but relaxed.

3) Take a deep breath in through your nose for four seconds.

4) Hold the breath for seven seconds.

5) Slowly breath out for eight seconds.

6) Repeat three to six times.

7) Notice how you are feeling.

Mindful breathing tells our brain to slow down. It can be particularly useful when dealing with anxiety or anger and can be utilized anywhere. Take time to practice this exercise often enough that it becomes second nature to use when you are experiencing anxiety or anger.

Chapter 15: Mindful Walking

After gaining some experience of practicing mindfulness through being mindful of breathing, sensations and feelings, you may have begun to notice mindfulness beginning to happen outside these practices. If so that's wonderful, if not, it will come in time. Either way Mindful walking is a great way to take your mindfulness practice on the move.

In mindful walking practice, you are going to apply what you have learned so far, while walking. Here I am going to break some of that down for you to initially work with specific senses. As with any mindfulness practice, your attention will wander at times, noticing this, is mindfulness in action.

There is no specified technique for mindful walking practice, other than applying the principles you have learned so far. I have seen some people do, and have dome myself, this practice walking extremely slowly, you may, but it isn't a requirement. Any pace but rushing will work fine. Indeed it is interesting to play with noticing if there is a speed that is optimal to maintain mindfulness and to notice what exactly happens at different speeds when mindfulness is lost or becomes something else.

Sensations

In this first mode of walking practice you will concentrate on bodily sensations. You might do this in whatever way appeals to you and I will offer a few suggestions and give some pointers.

A great place to start is the soles of your feet. Paying attention to exactly what sensations your feet are experiencing as you walk. Where does the sole first come into contact with the ground? How do you shift your weight through the step as you move forward? Does your foot roll slightly to the outside or inside edge? Is this different for each foot? So just in the same way as you have practiced being mindful of the body breathing, bring the same depth of attention to the sensations of the soles of your feet as you walk.

You could then possibly begin to move your attention upward through the body, to the ankles, shins/calves, knees, thighs taking time to notice attentively the sensations in each as you walk. You could continue this up through your body until finally you are paying attention to the sensations of your scalp as you walk.

You could then incorporate mindfulness of breathing as you walk, and later begin to hold awareness of the whole body field of sensations. You can really play with this in whatever way you wish in an open intention of curiosity. Finally pay attention to how you feel around the different sensations as you move through the body, noticing, accepting.

Hearing

In this next mode of walking practice you will concentrate on your sense of hearing. You may choose to focus at first on particular sounds, noticing the direction from which they come and all their qualities and how they change as you walk. Then allowing your attention to be drawn to a new sound and so on.

Having practiced focusing on particular sounds, you could try doing the same things and this time being also receptive to gently holding the other sounds that are there in your awareness.

From this you might move to a non-focused awareness of the field of sounds in your awareness, near to far, soft to loud, high to low, including the sounds you are making as you walk. Simply allowing all the sounds to register and bathe you in a more global experience of sound.

Throughout, pay attention to how you feel and respond to the different qualities of sound as you walk through this soundscape, noticing, accepting.

Scents

Our sense of smell of all the senses has the fastest route to the brain going directly to the limbic region. The limbic region is one of the more ancient parts of the brain sometimes called the mammalian brain and is strongly associated with our emotions and memory. This is why smells can be so powerfully evocative.

That said, our sense of smell might prove more allusive to be mindful of, depending on where you take it for a walk. Give it a go and see what our experience is.

As ever pay attention to not only what smells you sense as you walk and also pay attention to how you feel around the different qualities of scent, even stopping to notice what is evoked inside you as you do, noticing and accepting.

Seeing

Sight for many of us is a dominant sense, which is one reason I have left it until last. Hopefully having practiced walking mindful of sensations, sounds and smells will prove helpful in bringing mindfulness to what you see as you walk.

One of the first things you might notice is the automatic tendency of your mind to label, name or comment on what is seen. One potential way to overcome this strong habit is to soften and broaden the gaze. In doing this, the landscape becomes more a picture of different colors, shapes, textures and qualities of light. Personally, I really like to do this when I am walking somewhere that affords a large expansive view of the sky. The tones of blue and patterns, shapes and textures of cloud are limitless and ever changing. I find a similar experience walking in forests and woods where the multitude of tones and textures of greens and browns allows the sight to soften it's ever seeking gaze and instead allow the scene to enter into the eye.

It is probably a good idea to begin walking mindfulness with seeing, in such a natural landscape, before taking it into more everyday environments. When you do however, you will start to notice the mental-stream responding to what you are seeing. When this happens, allow awareness of the thoughts arising but rather than follow it down the mind-stream, see if you can become aware of the feelings beneath it. You might for example notice a feeling somewhere along the attraction – repulsion axis. Treat your own inner workings with a kindly curiosity and see what you notice in the interplay between, feeling, thought and emotion.

All together

Once you have spent some time practicing with each of these senses alone and gained some familiarity with mindfully walking with them, you can try playing with them in combinations or even a total sense feel of them all. It takes some practice to be able to hold this broader field awareness and it is very interesting when you can. I remember one evening once, meditating on a beach in southern India. I was practicing this open field mindful awareness, the sound of the waves, the touch of the wind, and opening myself to become the experience of the field of sounds, sensations and feelings. I noticed the wind growing stronger but practicing with closed eyes I wasn't aware it was because a thunderstorm was blowing in from the sea. In this open expansive and receptive state, I felt a sudden sharp jolt in my body. In that instant I opened my eyes to see the trace of a lightning bolt out over the ocean as the storm rushed closer. The lightning had been some distance away but I had <u>felt</u> it in the field of awareness very tangibly in my body.

Conclusion

I hope this book was able to help you to practice mindfulness techniques to reduce or eliminate your daily stress.

As you practice what you have learned, you will find that mindfulness will bring you many benefits including improved health on all levels as it brings your mind to the present and makes you truly aware of what is happening within your mind while your body is in action.

Mindfulness will also allow you to find the source of your stress and the right solution for it by being one with your environment, and knowing how your body and mind react to objects that you are surrounded with.

The next step to take is to practice each of the suggestions you've learned. Try each one out for a couple of weeks to learn which work the best for you. From that point you can develop your own techniques to relax by simply applying the idea of mindfulness in your daily activities.

Thank you again and best wishes for your mindful new life!

www.ingramcontent.com/pod-product-compliance
Lightning Source LLC
Chambersburg PA
CBHW072009070526
44583CB00015B/1405